Jesus the teacher

Story by Penny Frank

Illustrated by John Haysom

Guideposts

35

CARMEL • NEW YORK 10512

The Bible tells us how God sent his Son Jesus to show us what God is like and how we can belong to God's kingdom.

Jesus loved to talk about God's kingdom and explain it to his followers. In your own Bible, in Matthew's Gospel, chapters 5, 6 and 7, you will find some of the things he said.

Copyright © 1987 Lion Publishing

Published by
Lion Publishing plc
Icknield Way, Tring, Herts, England
Lion Publishing Corporation
1705 Hubbard Avenue, Batavia,
Illinois 60510, USA
Albatross Books Pty Ltd
PO Box 320, Sutherland, NSW 2232, Australia

First edition 1987
Reprinted 1987

Printed and bound in Hong Kong by Mandarin Offset Marketing (HK) Ltd
This Guideposts edition is published by special arrangement with Lion Publishing

British Library Cataloguing in Publication Data

Frank, Penny
Jesus the teacher.—(The Lion Story Bible; 35)
1. Jesus Christ—Teachings – Juvenile literature 2. Bible stories, English—N.T. Gospels
I. Title   II. Haysom, John
232.9'54   BS2416

Library of Congress Cataloging in Publication Data

Frank, Penny.
Jesus the teacher.
(The Lion Story Bible; 35)
1. Jesus Christ—Teachings—Juvenile literature. 2. Kingdom of God—Biblical teaching—Juvenile literature. 3. Bible stories, English—N.T. Matthew.
[1. Jesus Christ—Teachings. 2. Kingdom of God. 3. Bible stories—N.T.]
I. Haysom, John, ill. II. Title. III. Series: Frank, Penny. Lion Story Bible; 35.
BS2417.K5F73 1987   226'.209505
86-4704

One day, when Jesus had gone for a walk in the hills with his friends, he said to them, 'Listen carefully. I have some really important things to tell you. You will need to remember them when I am not with you any more.'

'It's no good thinking that God's kingdom is like this world,' said Jesus. 'If you asked the people you know what would make them happy, they would say being rich, or healthy, or famous.

'But I say there is happiness in God's kingdom for everyone, even those who are poor and ill and unimportant. The secret of real happiness is to love God and to do as he says.

'God wants you to pray to him. You can talk to him like this:
Our Father in heaven,
May we always show you respect.
We do want your kingdom to come on this earth, and your laws to be kept here, just as they are in heaven.
Please give us today the food that we need.
Forgive us for the wrong things we have done, and help us to forgive people who have hurt us and made us sad.
When Satan tries to make us disobey you, please help us not to do wrong.

'God is listening, even if he doesn't answer at once,' Jesus said. 'If you knock at someone's door and no one comes, you knock again. You go on knocking until the door is opened. So don't give up with God.

'Suppose you asked me for something and I didn't give it to you at once. Wouldn't you ask again? Well, prayer is like that. Don't be afraid to go on asking.

'In God's kingdom,' Jesus said, 'all the laws are good. There is a special law about loving people. Usually people like their friends and are unkind to their enemies.

'But God wants you to love even the people who hurt you. Then everyone will see that you belong to his kingdom.

'Don't always be on the lookout for things you don't like in other people. If you find fault with them they will soon turn around and point out your faults, too. In fact, don't be proud of yourself at all.

'Once upon a time a man stood in God's temple and prayed like this: "Dear God, I am so glad that I am good and keep all your laws." He was very proud.

'Another man prayed: "Dear God, please forgive me for all the wrong things I have done."

'It was that man who went home happy, for God forgave him.

'If you belong to God's kingdom, you don't have to worry about anything, ever again,' Jesus said. 'Look at those birds up there. If God makes sure they have food and drink, why should you feel worried about your next meal?

'As for new clothes — look at these
beautiful flowers, growing wild in the
field. God has given them clothes fit for
a king. He will make sure you have the
clothes you need, too.

'You want to have so many things,' Jesus said. 'And when you have them you worry about losing them. Perhaps they will get spoiled, or burglars will steal them.

'But if you belong to God's kingdom you know that the things you have don't matter very much. Your real treasure is in heaven. And there are no burglars there!

'Let's suppose there are two men, setting to work to build their new homes.

'The first one builds on solid rock. He works hard to make the foundations strong. Then he builds the walls. It takes a long time, but it's worth it.

'When the wind blows and the storms come and the river overflows, the house is safe. It is firm and strong on the rock.

'If you listen to me and do as I say, you are like that man.

'The second man wants to get the job done quickly. He chooses a place where the ground is soft and sandy and easy to dig. His house is soon built.

'But when the wind blows and the
storms come and the river overflows, the
sandy ground is washed away. Then the
house falls with a terrible crash. It can't
stay there without strong foundations.

'If you listen to me but do not do as I
say, you are like that man.

'I want you to be like bright lamps,'
Jesus said. 'When you light a lamp, you
don't cover it up, do you? Of course not.
You put it where it will give light to the
whole room. You are like light for the
world.

'I want you to be like a city built on top of a hill. People can see it for miles around. When they see the kind things you do, everyone will know that you belong to God's kingdom.'

The Story Bible Series from Guideposts is made up of 50 individual stories for young readers, building up an understanding of the Bible as one story—God's story—a story for all time and all people.

The Old Testament story books tell the story of a great nation—God's chosen people, the Israelites—and God's love and care for them through good times and bad. The stories are about people who knew and trusted God. From this nation came one special person, Jesus Christ, sent by God to save all people everywhere.

The New Testament story books cover the life and teaching of God's Son, Jesus. The stories are about the people he met, what he did and what he said. Almost all we know about the life of Jesus is recorded in the four Gospels—Matthew, Mark, Luke and John. The word gospel means 'good news.'

The last four stories in this section are about the first Christians, who started to tell others the 'good news,' as Jesus had commanded them—a story which continues today all over the world.

Jesus the Teacher is from the New Testament: Matthew's Gospel, chapters 5–7, the 'Sermon on the Mount.' This is the teaching Jesus gave to his disciples, out on the hillside above Lake Galilee, with a great crowd listening in. He turned the world's values upside down. What matters is not status, or possessions, or wealth, but whether or not we put God first in our lives. If our priorities are right, we can trust him for all we need. We can call him 'our Father.'